The Mindfulness Book

The Practical Meditation Book to Relieve Stress, Find Peace, and Cultivate Gratitude

Blair Abee

Energetic Wave Publishing
Vallejo, California

Blair Abee/Energetic Wave Publishing
139 Dyer Ct.
Vallejo, Ca. 94591
www.HiCMeditation.com

Book Layout ©2017 BookDesignTemplates.com v1

Ordering Information:
Quantity sales. Special discounts are available on quantity purchases by corporations, associations, and others. For details, contact the "Special Sales Department" at the address above.

The Mindfulness Book, Blair Abee. —1st ed.
ISBN   978-1-   737283904

Contents

Hello, or is This Book for You? 5

Meditation 13

Quickies: Six Second Meditations 23

Sacred Breathing...25

Sacred Words and Phrases--Mantras...........................35

Sacred Speaking 55

Mudra Meditations 59

Some Other "Quickies" 63

Conclusion: How and Why 65

Next Steps 73

Sacred Senses..77

Another Poem...91

ABOUT THE AUTHOR...94

Energetic Wave Publishing Resources for You

These are worrisome and stressful times. Meditation and Higher Consciousness is your path to freedom and abundance. Blair offers a number of resources to you the reader to help you on your Journey to Illumination, Soul Contact, and freedom from the human condition.

His **complete book list** at Amazon includes:

- The Many Amazing Benefits of Meditation: Living the Life You've Always Wanted to Live
- The Meditation Book: The Essential Meditation for Beginners to Find Peace, Reduce Stress, and Improve Mental Health
- The Mindfulness Book: The Practical Meditation Book to Relieve Stress, Find Peace, and Cultivate Gratitude
- The Abundance Book: The Spiritual Path to Abundance (available September 2021)
- Homage to Spirit: Poems to Elevate Consciousness

In addition, he offers **a 6-hour class** on "Meditation and Abundance" every other month, covering:

- Sit-down meditation using his Higher Consciousness Meditation process
- Mindfulness meditation using his Higher Consciousness Mindfulness exercises
- Creating abundance from a spiritual perspective
- Health and wellness, with meditation and other techniques to create optimum health

Contact him for the next class at Blair@HigherConsciousnessMeditation.com.

For those interested in **one-on-one meditation and awareness consultation** Blair offers 1 hour coaching sessions. Contact him at Blair@HigherConsciousnessMeditation.com.

His **website** HiCMeditation.com is chock full of information about Higher Consciousness Meditation topics:

- A blog with in-depth articles about meditation topics and wellness issues
- Sample chapters of his books
- Spiritual poems
- A curated shopping area for products he recommends to help you create a healthy home environment with high vibrational qualities—things he and his wife have and love in their home
- A newsletter signup

Lastly, you can get a morning inspirational quote/picture in your Facebook, Instagram or Twitter feed by going to https://www.facebook.com/authormeditation, https://www.instagram.com/hicmeditation/ or https://twitter.com/AbeeBlair. 365 **Daily Vibes** will make you smile and lift up for a year.

CHAPTER 1

Hello, or is This Book for You?

Take a moment as you open this book to do a quick exercise. Take a deep breath. Say to yourself, "Peace, be still". Take another breath and feel the effect of doing this. You have just done a six second meditation; a mindfulness exercise.

If this felt good, if it enlivened you, keep reading. That is what this book is about. Raising your vibration with quick pauses throughout the day intended to shift your consciousness to a higher state.

Why? Doing so results in a better life and a greater sense of well-being if we make it a practice to frequently use mindfulness exercises and incorporate them into our daily lives.

Why? Because our experiences in life are dramatically affected by our state of mind, our state of consciousness, our vibrational frequency (more about this later).

Our thoughts and our state of mind is just about the only thing we have total, complete control over. We don't have to let our thoughts, feelings, or moods run away with us., and it's important, therefore, that we take care of that state of mind to raise ourselves up to the level of our best possible Selves, even to our Eternal Selves, as frequently as possible. Quickie meditations are one of the optimal ways to do that.

It has been said many times in many ways, "We can't control the things that happen to us, but we can control our reactions to them." I would argue that we can have control both over the things that happen to us <u>and</u> our reactions to them. (I'll address the issue of our control over things that happen to us at the end of Chapter 2.) The best way to control your reactions to things that happen in your world is to pause a moment, take a deep breath and do a six second meditation intended to interject your desired vibration into your reaction.

From my own personal experience, I use the techniques/tools that are discussed in this book for a variety of purposes:
- To brighten up my morning as I wake up.
- To begin my yoga and meditation practices
- To be grateful for the Life that I will experience during my day.
- To be thankful for the entire system that produced my breakfast.
- To enliven the run Sasha dog and I take every morning.
- To interrupt the momentum of a cold that might be making an appearance.
- To offer a healing thought to the news I'm watching.
- To appreciate the financial resources, I have
- To bless my writing

The trick to this way of life is remembering. Remembering to remember to take a moment, a pause, a breath.

A two second breath or a six second meditation to go Within can put me right in touch with my Soul, or Higher Consciousness, with which many of us are not very well acquainted. Yet, I contend, this is where well-being and the spiritual qualities of love, joy, peace, contentment, compassion, healing, abundance (and more) reside—Within.

Some examples:
- In traffic, you can take a deep breath and say "peace, be still" rather than "I hate you, faceless other driver" or "I hate being stuck in traffic" or "I hate my circumstances that puts me in this situation" or "Damn, I'm going to be late" or..... whatever you say that sets up an angry, upset state of mind reaction to your circumstances.

  Why not take charge of your own state of mind, your self-talk, and have a peaceful experience in traffic instead of a yucky one. The traffic is the traffic. There's little you can do about traffic when you are in it, but you can control what occupies your attention when you are there--turning on a lovely bit of music, singing to yourself, listening to an uplifting talk from a masterful teacher or your favorite novelist, inhaling a Sacred Breath, or imagining what you would do with this time if you weren't stuck behind a delivery truck.
- First thing in the morning, before getting out of bed, take a few seconds to take a deep breath and say to yourself, "What a wonderful world. Thank you, Spirit, for Life,".

This will set the tone for your whole day but requires that you take responsibility for your state of mind by being thankful for Life itself; using mind and soul to alter your well-worn patterns.

Being grumpy in the morning isn't your only option. You may have said to yourself over and over again a thousand times, "I'm not a morning person". But that statement only true if you say that it is and believe it. With a little bit of effort and awareness you can replace that self-talk and personal vibration with anything you want. How about "First thing in the morning is a sacred time for me and I see the beauty of it".

Gives your morning a whole different story line. It's up to you.

This book is about an updated you. Although you are perfect just the way you are, there is a whole other you that this book will explore. An illumined you. An incredible you that you know is inside of you but which many people don't have much access to.

Unfortunately, most of us have never been exposed to the real meaning of Gautama Siddhartha Buddha's words, "This (Enlightenment) that I have attained is profound, hard to see and hard to understand, peaceful and sublime, unattainable by mere reasoning, subtle, to be experienced by the wise".

I wasn't exposed to Buddha in my formative years in Charlotte, North Carolina. No emphasis was placed, in the Lutheran Church I grew up in, on these words of Jesus words that still ring through the centuries, "*The kingdom of God does not come with observation; nor will they say, 'See here!' or 'See there!'* **For indeed, the kingdom of God is within you".** I don't remember a single sermon, in all the years I went to church on Sunday and Wednesday, which addressed this, and his other cornerstone of his message, "I and the Father are One".

The words of the prophet Mohammed are similar, *"Thou art a mortal being, And thou art the Eternal One. Know thyself, through the light of wisdom. Except Thee there exists none* "were unknown to me. He was a pagan, to the extent he was mentioned at all in the Christian world, and unworthy of discussion.

Why? I think because no spiritual leader that I was ever exposed to knew what the words of either of these two meant. Therefore, Jesus' most important ideas were never mentioned. Instead, in the much of the Christian church world, Jesus is said to be the only Son of God that ever existed and at the extreme, a non-believer in Him has no hope of ever entering heaven. In this latter teaching, heaven's gates are guarded by a saint and access to the man with a white beard who rules the universe from a throne is available only to those who "confess Jesus as Lord".

This rather.... gosh what word do I use? This rather.... limited view of what Jesus was about has condemned his followers to a Heaven that is only accessible after they die. The man clearly said, "The Kingdom of God (Heaven), in inside of you". That means all of us, not just some. This means that all of us have access to Heaven now. Here.

If we come to realize and experiences these things, we will be following Jesus' example, Buddha's example, Mohammed's example, and the example of others of our Master Teachers, who had their own personal experience of this phenomenon. And honoring their memories by following their examples.

So how do we get access to this Kingdom, this Nirvana, this state of Illumination which our Master Teachers have spoken of from their own personal experience?

What do their words mean and how can we get access to the same experience, Higher Consciousness? How can we grow our spiritual Selves as well as improve our daily lives?

That's what we will explore in this volume, which is relatively short compared to some of my other books. I'll give you some ideas and tools to journey in that direction of Illumination if you are so inclined. I can't promise complete Enlightenment, but I can promise that you can have glimpses of it, which you can then choose to pursue in your own way. In addition, you can dramatically improve your sense of well-being and the quality of your life.

Questions to Consider.

1. What type of spiritual upbringing did you have? Did it ever mention the availability of Spirit Within?

2. Have you had experiences since then that have caused you to consider this question of Spirit Within?

3. What do you now think about this idea? Do you like it? Would you be interested in exploring it further?

CHAPTER 2

Meditation

I'm writing this book as a companion to my book <u>The</u> <u>Meditation Book</u>. In it I reveal a new, powerful process called Higher Consciousness Meditation for doing a potent, exciting, fun, six-minute meditation. If you haven't read that book and tried the process, go to Amazon Kindle and get a copy.

I realized, however, that while I love longer meditations (it's where I get my daily "juice"), the gut of life is lived in the moment-by-moment interactions that we have with the world and ourselves--what we think, how we respond, what we do. It's in these moments that life is lived out and that my awareness and my body/mind/personality is played out.

I also realized that I have near complete control over all of that, and that it was my responsibility to unfold the day to day in the way I want to. Consistent with my desire to be as aware and effective in the world I live in as I could be.

To do this, therefore, was going to require that I spend as much time in an aware, mindful state as possible and to do that I needed to develop some additional tools. The tools had to be practical and useful. They began to emerge out of the clues that I had gathered over the years from my study of spiritual matters.

Some of these techniques discussed in this volume are offshoots of ideas from other people and even quotes from other sources. I have also used what I know about human nature and adult learning to develop my own techniques. I began to chronicle some of these tools in the previous book but realized that the subject needed the full attention of an accompanying book.

Lastly, it became clear to me that the tools had to be "quick bites"; strategies and approaches to life's daily problems and personal issues that could be applied in real time. My quest was dramatically aided by the close relative to "sit down" meditation—mindfulness meditation.

In my view, both sit-down and mindfulness meditation practices are needed by the serious student/practitioner of meditation. Sit-down meditation, done once or twice a day gives us a chance to spend 5-15 minutes to just rest in our Essence and experience the beauty of being awash in Spirit. Mindfulness exercises done throughout the day, on the other hand, is a refresher, a quick tune-up/tune in to that Essence, especially when stressful situations come along. Together they have the potential for creating a sustained elevation of consciousness that can be built on day by day until we find ourselves transformed in our Awareness and our Locus of Attention.

What is Meditation? Why Do It?
Let's start by defining meditation and delve a little deeper.

(Some of this same information is given in my previous book Higher Consciousness Meditation.)

According to Wikipedia:

"Meditation is a practice in which an individual trains the mind or induces a mode of consciousness, either to realize some benefit or as an end in itself

The term *meditation* refers to a broad variety of practices (much like the term *sports*) that includes techniques designed to promote relaxation, build internal energy or life force (*qi*, *ki*, *prana*, etc.) and develop compassion, love, patience, generosity and forgiveness.

Meditation often involves an internal effort to self-regulate the mind in some way. Meditation is often used to clear the mind and ease many health issues, such as high blood pressure, depression, and anxiety. It may be done sitting, or in an active way. For instance, Buddhist monks (and others, ed.) involve awareness (called 'mindfulness", ed.) in their day-to-day activities as a form of mind-training."

Mindfulness Meditation

Also, according to Wikipedia, 'right mindfulness' is the seventh element of Buddha's noble eightfold path. He considered mindfulness to be an antidote to delusion and a 'power', or ability, which contributes to the attainment of *nirvana*, or a state of perfect peace.

Over the years different people have developed mindfulness techniques intended to help reach that state of perfect peace. And if not perfect peace, imperfect peace.

This faculty becomes a power, in particular, when it is coupled with a clear awareness of whatever is taking place, right here and right now. In a state of perfect peace mental jibber jabber, stress, greed, hatred, and delusion are overcome and abandoned, and are absent from the mind.

Mindfulness induces a state of "moment to moment non-judgmental awareness" using, among other things, thought and breath observation, body scanning, mindful walking, and being aware of the taste and texture of the food that we eat.

The short six second mindfulness practices presented in this book are designed to put us back into a place of peace and contact with our Soul. To, if only for a moment, remind us of who we are, an Eternal Being, thereby making it easier to cope with the world and to grow into our Higher Selves.

Some Additional "Whys?"

I'd like to offer some additional ideas about why both longer and shorter meditations are of value. The key "why?" boils down to one word: vibration.

My research indicates that Gautama Buddha was one of the first to assert this when he said, "All that we are is the result of what we have thought; it is founded on our thoughts; it is made up of our thoughts. A man's life is the direct result of his thoughts…

We are what we think. All that we are arises with our thoughts. With our thoughts we make the world."

To Buddha's teaching, I would add that the sum total of our mental, along with emotional, physical, and spiritual states contributes to the vibrational "cloud" that surrounds each of us. This cloud is made up a swirl of energy that attracts the good and the bad into our lives, based on our thoughts, feelings, actions, karma, and spiritual beliefs. This cloud creates our own unique, individualized universe.

Our daily lives, then, are the "outpicturing" of the vibrations we embody in conformity with the Laws of Vibration and Attraction which state, fundamentally, that "like attracts like".

The mindfulness techniques offered in this book are intended to help us raise the vibration in our physical, mental, emotional, and spiritual "bodies" so that the life that we and our Soul, together, outpicture is the best that it can be.

Note that I said, "we and our Soul, together". In my experience, my Soul or Higher Consciousness has become an integral part of the life of my human self. I feel this Presence constantly, talk to Him (since I am a man), and HiC, as I affectionately refer to Him, often seems to be flowing through my fingers and right onto this keyboard that I write with.

HiC began to emerge as something "real" as I went deeper into my meditation practice about 5 years ago. Now we are inseparable.

And Now, The Benefits

The beauty of meditation is its positive impact on the human experience. In my book, The Amazing Benefits of Meditation, I point out how almost every day new scientific research emerges to reveal what mystics and meditators have known for centuries—meditation improves our physical, mental, emotional, and spiritual well-being.

Studies have been done over the past 20 or more years that show that these, and many more conditions, respond to meditation. For example, meditation, among many other things:

- Reduces risk of **heart disease and stroke**
- **Decreases pain**
- Improves **focus, attention, concentration, and multitasking** ability
- Gives us mental **strength, resilience** and **emotional intelligence**
- **Boosts happiness and optimism**
- **Reduces emotional eating**

Why Does This Happen? How Can This Be?

Scientists are less clear about the "why?" and "how?" meditation works than about the fact that it does. This leaves to us who study the subject of meditation deeply and comb the writings of mystics, as well as personally research these questions, to develop our own answers.

Many of the undesirable conditions listed above get started and become chronic because the ego/body/mind gets caught in a loop of cause, effect, cause, effect until a momentum gets generated that self-perpetuates the problem that arises from.....who knows where.. Conditions, like the ones listed above and others, respond, or more accurately, recede, by interrupting the flow of the condition with a pause and a break in the momentum of the condition.

This is, of course, what meditation does. It interrupts the ego/body/mind, especially the mind, in its relentless pursuit of thought, thought, thought, worry, worry, worry, remembrances of past difficult situations, and anticipation of future ones.

Churning, churning, churning. This is the mind's job, it seems, especially in times of threat. Meditation interrupts this cycle, calms the mind, assuages the ego, and relaxes the body. The whole system takes a bit of a break, and the body's natural healing mechanism, which tends toward well-being, kicks in.

Can Meditation's Benefits be Amplified?

The next logical question that occurred to me is "Can the interruption of 'the loop' be amplified and made stronger". I think so. In fact, I think that is what Master Teachers who were healers did. By amplifying their own healing energy, they were able to interrupt the flow of their patients' conditions, allow Spirit to flow, and cause healing to occur.

I offer a number of options in this book that can be used for specific purposes: mindfulness techniques, mantras, mudras, and others that we can use to take advantage of the benefits meditation offers.

Of course, not all conditions respond to meditation, and modern medicine is frequently needed. Conditions from a broken bone to a broken childhood may require the assistance of a trained medical expert. Even here, though, from my personal experience, mediation can be beneficial.

My theory about that is that the right kind of meditation can cause the physical body, mental body and/or emotional body, when Spirit begins to flow, to increase our internal rate of vibration and, thereby, raise the vibration of the effected element of the human system. Interrupting the "loop" as well as improving the strength of the medical approach being used.

For this reason, I always do a short meditation, a mindfulness exercise, to improve the efficacy of the medicine I might be taking for a short term or long-term condition. I have the beginnings of macular degeneration, for example, and take eye medicine to address the problem medically. Ever since I began my medicine/meditation routine, my condition has ceased to get worse, according to the ophthalmologist. I usually accompany my pill swallowing by saying to myself, "Peace, be still".

One More, Very Important, Thing

Improving our lives, then, involves changing our consciousness rather than the quality of our thoughts, our subconscious drives, or our word prayers. The Higher Consciousness Meditation techniques, both the longer traditional "sit down" technique and short mindfulness techniques herein involves aligning with our Souls to raise our vibratory rate.

Higher Consciousness Meditation techniques cause our point of attention to become more Spirit oriented; more of our daily thoughts and impulses are generated at the Soul level. These spiritualized Thoughtforms register in our mind, flow through into our feelings and body, and out into our world of experience.

Their higher vibration "amps up" the atmosphere surrounding us and attracts to us higher-level experiences. Our life can change dramatically in a short period of time if we are able to make the transition from generating lower-level thoughts and vibrations to higher frequency ones. Five second meditations are intended to help do that.

Questions to Consider
What do you think of these ideas? Do they seem radical?
Does it make sense that a physical, mental, or emotional condition that you have might have something to do with the thoughts and vibrational frequency that you may be generating?

How about the idea that you can interrupt the "loop" that results from such thoughts and vibrations with meditation?

CHAPTER 3

Quickies: Six Second Meditations

These quick, Six Second Meditations (SSMs) can put us directly into a state of Higher Consciousness. (I hope you are beginning to see that Higher Consciousness is nothing mysterious. It's available at any moment you turn to it and SSMs are great ways to do that.)

Try them. Day to day, moment to moment, these techniques can be used almost anytime, anywhere, under any circumstance without bothering others but greatly benefitting us. Each time we go Within and use an SSM, our vibration takes jump, we "vibe up" at least for a moment, and our Awareness shifts. Over time these jumps contribute to small but, incremental, internal, and potentially, permanent personal changes.

Browse through these offerings and make notes of a few you want to try right away. Others you may want to save for later. Some won't suit you at all. In any case, you won't be able to do them all at the same time. That would be too much, too soon—information overload. Instead, experiment. Find out what works for you. Keep in mind that something that seems helpful today may fade in its efficacy over time—you may successfully internalize the lesson of one now and need a new one later. One approach may get boring and need to be replaced with another.

There is a variety here to keep you busy for quite some time. Many of you, however, will become creative and develop your own mindfulness exercises to remind yourself to remember to stay Awake. If you do, please share them with the rest of the community on our Higher Consciousness Meditation website.

For ease of use I have put the techniques into four groups in the next few chapters: Sacred Breathing, words, and phrases (word triggers), mudras (hand gestures) and "others".

Questions to Consider

Only one. And I assume the fact that you are still reading this at least means the answer is "maybe". Are you going to try this a bit and see what happens?

CHAPTER 4

Sacred Breathing

My favorite six second meditation is Sacred Breathing. It takes very little time to pause and take a breath that has a particular purpose determined by our intent. Sacred Breaths are certainly a way to raise our consciousness, the vibration of our Being, and they are a key component of the longer HCM process described in the <u>Higher Consciousness Meditation</u> book.

In summary, a Sacred Breath is taken by inhaling and letting Spirit expand our consciousness, pausing for a moment to let It pool up and then letting the Spirit breath flow out into our world. Doing so enlivens us <u>and</u> the world around us.

Part of the value of Sacred Breathing is that it is a tool to be used over and over again to soothe the human body/mind/personality and help it get comfortable with a transformation that begins to take place. A transformation in which our Spirit Mind begins to be more "in charge" and our whole system begins operating at a higher level of vibration.

I remember when this higher level was new to me, intriguing and a bit scary to my mind as I observed my mind's reaction to the new kid on the block. I liken this to our 8-year-old cat's reaction to the new kitten that recently appeared in our lives. Annie Cat acted intimidated and intimidating with 5-week-old Cleo. She did not like the change and acted very territorial with the little one: hissing and growling and puffing up.

There was no justification for this except that it was Annie's natural reaction to change, much like our human mind when something new is introduced into its system. Slowly Annie learned that there was no threat, that this new creature was harmless. Perhaps, as my wife Lynne speculates, on some level she knew that this was a baby feline, worthy of mothering. Annie got used to the little one and now when we go on a 3-day trip, and leave the two of them together alone, she has company and does not miss us as much. (Outcome: Annie adopted Cleo. My human mind is still slowly adopting my Spirit Mind.)

Sacred Breathing is one of the most powerful of all of the spiritual tools available if we learn how to use it properly. Here are some of the ways:

- As a quick trigger to raise our vibration any time we use it. Start by saying to yourself, "I take a **Higher Consciousness Breath**," and take a long, slow breath with Higher Consciousness in mind. This will immediately put you into a different state of mind. It can be used anytime, anywhere. Silently. Nobody else needs to know.

  I have used this exercise in many different situations. For example, I will take a Sacred Breath just before doing just about any task: starting a meeting, beginning a difficult conversation, serving a tennis ball. It enriches the moment and puts me into a better frame of mind to accomplish the task.

- As a consciousness shifter while doing a repetitious, frightening, or physical task: when digging a ditch, having my teeth drilled on, or cooking. I think my fish always tastes better and has more love cooked into it when I practice Sacred Breathing.

- As subconscious mind breathing. We each have a part of our minds, known as the subconscious mind, where we have urges below our conscious awareness. This concept of was originally developed and popularized by Sigmund Freud. Since its introduction, empirical evidence suggests that subconscious mind phenomena include repressed feelings, automatic skills, subliminal perceptions, thoughts, habits, automatic reactions, and, possibly, complexes, hidden phobias and desires, and repressed memories of painful incidents.

I have found it helpful to breathe into that part of myself when it is activated or active in my behavior. Recently, for example, I woke up with a feeling in the pit of my stomach. Fear. I didn't recognize it at first, thinking it might be indigestion (which I never get). I spent 15 minutes in bed recognizing the fear and dissolving it, reaching for some good feelings, using my meditation techniques. Nothing much worked.

I got up, did my usual yoga routine, and spent about twenty minutes in an intense meditation--really using Sacred Breathing, focused on breathing into the pit of my stomach. The fear began to subside and the "aha" moment came. I had gone to bed without meditating the night before, and after listening to a webinar that ended with the usual "scarcity" scenario; "If you don't buy this product before midnight, you will lose out". I wasn't even that interested in the product, a software solution to a problem I didn't have. My subconscious mind, however, had been hooked by the message.

A few more Sacred Breaths and my consciousness began to move in the direction of Awareness and my vibration rate rose. The fear subsided and was replaced by an eagerness for the day, by a sense of feeling good, by a feeling of lightness. It was with this that I was able to begin the day, which was much fun. Lynne and I went shopping and found some great plants for the yard. I worked in my office for a while and some pieces of a project fell into place. All in all, it was a good day.

(As I write this, I'm reminded to avoid watching scary movies, or anything else that is fear-based before I go to bed—they lodge in my subconscious mind and my dreams are often troubled when I do.)

Another time, Lynne pointed out to me that I was speaking to a person in our Tai Chi class in the same overbearing way my father used to use. It never worked for him very well, but I think I learned it from him, and it sometimes comes out in inappropriate ways. That evening I spent a while breathing in a sacred way into that part of me where the behavior was lodged, and I have been able to catch myself several times recently before repeating that undesirable behavior.

- As a trigger for involving my Higher Consciousness, my Soul. On another occasion I was inspired to say "Breathe me and through me HiC. Breathe me and be me. Fill my very lungs with Spirit." I felt the intake of Spirit and the exhale of Spirit, into my world and into Eternity. I thought, "All I have to do is do this and I am filled with Light." It was this incident that led me to include Sacred Breathing as a key part of Higher Consciousness Mindfulness.

Here are some other uses that can be made of Sacred Breathing. The key is intent. The technique can be coupled with sacred words and phrases, like "Peace, Be Still" mentioned in earlier. When taking a Sacred Breath, pause for a moment and listen to see if your Soul has anything to add to the silence and the vibrational upsurge.

Here's what I mean:

- A **Soul Breath** will take us to that individualized state of Higher Consciousness in which we can have a very intimate relationship with our Soul. My HiC is always awaiting my turning to It.

- An **Om Breath**. The word "Om" is said in Hinduism to be the sound of the vibration of the universe. Breathe in and say or intone "Om" on your exhale, drawing it out as long as possible.

- A **Go Within Breath** shifts our awareness from our body/mind/personality to our Spirit/Mind.

- A **(Love, Joy, Peace) Breath** puts us into attunement with that divine quality which we are wanting/needing to experience at a particular moment.

- A **Hug Breath** is great for experiencing the higher nature of a significant other or child and establishes Soul contact in a flash.

- A **Creative Breath** will tap into our creativity and can tap into that Higher Consciousness part of ourselves from which great thoughts and ideas flow.

- A **Transformation Breath** can be used to alter our perception of a situation or to transform the situation itself.

- A **Knowledge Breath** will, as with the Creative Breath, tap us into the Source of all knowledge, as well as help us remember where the car keys are.

- An **Appreciation Breath** can be used to internally express gratitude for anything, from a beautiful sunset to Life itself.

- A **Tiger Breath** can put us in touch with our place of Courage and Bravery. I take one of these before the chiropractor cracks my neck or the dentist begins his drilling, before making a difficult phone call or beginning a difficult conversation, or before going out on stage. For these types of situations, I use a **Peace Be Still Breath** if that is more appropriate in the moment.

- **Healing Breath**. This one has lots of uses: when getting unfavorable health news about yourself or others, when hurting yourself, when waking up to the flu or feeling nauseous, when taking medication or beginning a health procedure, when "bad things" happening in your presence, or when emotionally upsetting situations occur to you or others.

- **Compassion Breath**. As Gautama Buddha said (paraphrasing), this is a painful world, this 3-dimensional (3d) reality. A Compassion Breath for individuals or groups who are experiencing physical, mental, emotional, or spiritual pain can help you, them, and all of us. Include being compassionate with yourself. This and the other "breaths" listed here can elevate us to our Higher Consciousness, or to 5-Dimensional (5D) Reality.

- **Disagreement Breath**. Disagreements and upsets with others can be exceedingly difficult to deal with. When one of the parties, however, takes responsibility for handling a situation with a heightened form of awareness, it is possible for these types of tugs and pulls to be lessened, alleviated or an agreement to disagree established.

- **Karma Breath**. Mistakes, misjudgments, hurtful things that we think, say, or do to ourselves and to others create karma for ourselves and with others. Why not use a Karma Breath to adjust what will otherwise be a backlash upon us as a result?

- Use a **Forgiveness Breath** to forgive everyone and everything involved in any unconscious behavior that has occurred. Use the Breath to dissolve the effects of an action so that it is as if it never occurred. And act to right the wrong if possible.

- **Action or Performance Breath**. Take an Action Breath before or during the planning or execution of any action you want to bring Higher Consciousness to (most things, after all): driving in heavy traffic, athletic activities, teeth brushing, serving customers, working with colleagues, mowing the grass, bathing the baby, and countless others.

- **Food Breath**. Similar to the Action Breath this is done in the planning, cooking, and serving process. It will not only improve the quality of the food but cook love and awareness into our sustenance.

- **Eating Breath**. Food is meant to be enjoyed, appreciated, and well digested. Being conscious of our breath, eating slowly and thoroughly, savoring the food, appreciating the chain of "suppliers" who produced the food including the animals and plants who have given their lives for us, and all of the people who participated in the food's delivery will enliven our lives and make for good digestion, as well.

- **Plant/Animal/Thing Breath**. All things have vibration. This Breath enables us to see the Life Force in them, even rocks. Relationship, appreciation, and compassion for them can thereby be established. I use this when I escort spiders from the house with a Kleenex.

- **World Breath**. Our world is rife with problems, difficulties, atrocities, unconsciousness, and sad events. Take a Breath or two for this world and its inhabitants each day to lighten the load. Perhaps while you watch or listen to the news, and especially when something awful is presented. (See also **Compassion Breath**.)

- A **Sacred Breath** can be used for anything, including things not covered by this partial list.

Sacred Breathing is a lovely way to live. It enlivens us and the world around us. It can transform the difficulty of living on Planet Earth, including the twists and turns of our own internal makeup and circumstances. We just have to remember to use the tools.

Questions to Consider
What do you think, does Sacred Breathing seem like a good mindfulness exercise? Which one would you like to try first and why?

CHAPTER 5

Sacred Words and Phrases-- Mantras

"Mantra" is a "Sanskrit word which refers to a sacred utterance, sound, syllable, word, or group of words believed by some to have psychological and spiritual power," according to Wikipedia. A mantra may or may not have a literal meaning; the spiritual value comes when it is heard, seen or present in thought.

I like to think of a mantra as a word or phrase that elevates my awareness when said once or over and over with sacred intent. Mantras used this way enable me to go Within for a sacred moment, to shift my awareness from 3d to 5D consciousness and to raise my vibration. Without intent and Awareness mantras are useless to us as spiritual tools, just vain utterances. With Awareness and intent, they can be powerful centering, learning, remembering, and accomplishing tools.

The first one "Spirit and I are One" is one of my favorites and I use it all of the time: to change my valence, to quieten my mind when it has gone off on a tangent, to put myself into a state of

Awareness and/or to invite Spirit into the moment. Imagine if you said this to yourself and felt it for just an instant, once per hour, what it would do in your life. It changes everything.

These mantras are categorized based on use or purpose. Some are general purpose and can be used any time. Others are specific to particular circumstance. If you are facing a specific difficult situation, for example, use one from the Difficult Situation category.

Alternatively, you might have an issue or problem you want to work on for a while—a day, a week, or a month. In that case, consider a particular category as a "theme" and try out the various mantras until you perceive that a shift has occurred around that problem that satisfies you.

Instructions:
- Pause. Take a Sacred Breath by breathing in with the awareness that Spirit is expanding inside of you.
- Breathe out with the awareness that you are radiating Spirit into your world.
- Say one of the mantras below with the intent that you immediately transition into the state indicated by the mantra. Repeat if you need to and have the time.
- You should feel a shift in your awareness in the direction of the intent of the mantra you used. It may last for an instant or for a few moments or longer. The more you use them the better they work.
- This should not feel like "work", but more like Soul play. Have fun with it. Create your own mantras. Share them and your results with the community of folks who are working with these at HiCMeditation.com.

- Lastly, feel free to change the wording to suit your interests, your beliefs or your Soul's prompting.

The Mantras and Their Explanations

There is an introduction to each category and 4 examples, with explanatory notes.

- **General purpose**. Can be used any time. These are pretty self-explanatory. They are used to get centered, be in the moment and raise your vibration.

  "Spirit and I are One". This take off on Jesus' "I and the Father are One" indicates the same thing—that when you are in a state of Higher Consciousness, as Jesus was most of the time, you are one with The ALL, Spirit. Saying it alone, however, will not make it happen. You have to take that Sacred Breath and feel it. Let it rise up in you. Same with the rest of these.

  "Peace be still". Another Jesus saying, made to a storm he and his disciples were in on the Sea of Galilee. It just as easily be used to quieten the storm most of us experience in our minds.

  "I let go and let Spirit intervene". Living a conscious life can mean letting Spirit go before you to "make the crooked places straight". Letting go is the tough part of this mantra because the ego/mind does not want to.

  "I am present, here, now". Being present in the here and now is the essence of mindfulness. Another thing the ego/mind does not want to do. Read the classic Be Here, Now by Ram Das to get good training on this one.

"Delight in everything". This one flashed on me a few days ago and I have been using it 5-6 times a day since. Just saying it alters my state of consciousness and I <u>am</u> delighted by whatever is occurring in front of me. These things work!

- **Who Am I?** It's easy to get confused about who we are, a human being having a human experience and an Eternal Being having a human experience. The world and its goings on are so seductive that it is easy to forget and live life from our ego/mind rather than your Higher Consciousness. These should help you sort that out.

  "I Am that I Am" the thing which God was supposed to have said to Moses when he got the 10 Commandments. This one reminds me that Spirit, Allness, is, and that I Am One with It. The experience of omnipresence may occur.

  "I am whole and complete", something to remind yourself when your self-talk turns negative.

  "I am the master of my fate and the captain of my Soul", from the poem <u>Invictus</u> by William Ernest Henley. In the same poem he said, "I thank whatever gods may be for my unconquerable soul."

  "I am a beloved Son/Daughter of the God". Remember this one and you'll never go wrong.

- **What qualities do I want to experience?** As an Eternity Being we each have within us the same qualities as Spirit. These statements clearly and simply make that point, putting us in a state of vibration and "switching the channel" from what may not look so lovely to one from which lovely can be seen. These are hard to talk about but available to be experienced. (By saying "I am…." you claim that quality for yourself.)

"I Am Divine Love". Divine Love is the power of attraction in creation that harmonizes, unites, and binds together. It is unconditional, asks for nothing and gives everything. The state, or feeling, is what we are wanting with this one. When you give it, radiate it, you benefit yourself as well. My wife Lynne used this one extensively while going through chemotherapy.

"I Am Divine Joy". Joy describes being thrilled with the ecstasy of living, combining both serenity and excitement along with a touch of humor or laughter. Divine Joy takes us to a different dimension—5-Dimensional Reality.

"I Am Divine Peace". Divine Peace is a state of quiet, stillness, security and freedom from fear that cannot be understood with the mind, only experienced. It comes from the essence of you, not from circumstances.

"I have an Illumined Mind". Halos around the heads of Master Teachers depicted in art throughout the ages is a representation of an Illumined Mind—lit up by Spirit.

- **The ALL, God, Spirit, Source, Infinite Divine Intelligence mantras.** It is beneficial to frequently acknowledge the Source from which we spring. I'm not one to use the word "God" very much because it has so many different meanings and definitions to so many people based on their upbringings. Spirit, Source, Divine Intelligence work better for me as descriptors of that experience of The ALL from which all springs. The purpose of these sacred phrases is to use your Awareness to transcend your mind's desire to define everything and instead, put you into a state of direct communion with Source.

"The ALL is........ Here. Now". The ALL is a term that comes from the Hermetic tradition. Hermes said that ALL is in The ALL and The ALL is in ALL. Saying "The ALL is.... Ising" may be the closest one can get to saying nothing and everything. Deepak Chopra uses the word "Consciousness" to describe God, which has Awareness and "Ising" elements to it.

"I sense Omnipresence". The ALL is Presence being present everywhere at the same time and able to be sensed by our Soul. Stretch. One glimpse is stupendous.

"I am in touch with Spirit right now" is another way of saying the same thing.

"From Spirit I live out into the world". Here's the key to this group--sensing The ALL, sensing your Soul, and living out into the world from that Place.

- **Soul, individualized Higher Consciousness, HiC** (the reference I like to use for my Higher Consciousness) is the Eternal Companion with whom we were paired when we emerged from The ALL. Our growth in Awareness, at some point, makes it possible for us to have direct contact with this Self, and continue on in Divine Partnership with our Soul.

"Soul is.....Here, Now" acknowledges the existence of an Individualized Consciousness; One with The ALL but specific to us. A Guide and Companion, experienceable

will go up, if only a little. Do it several times and the result is often dramatic.

"My Soul and I transform the world I experience". Shifting our point of awareness to Higher Consciousness transforms the way we experience the world. It becomes more luminescent, and our higher vibration attracts to us higher quality experiences.

- **Consciousness/Awareness.** Our state of mind, our awareness, on our Soul journey becomes increasingly important, replacing other concerns. It is good to remind ourselves of what our priorities are.

"My state of my consciousness is the most important thing right now". With this we exercise our choice about what we place our attention on.

"I shift my attention from my ego/mind to my Spirit/ Mind". This is a key choice to make over and over.

"I rest back into my Higher Consciousness". This does not have to be a lot of work. In fact, it shouldn't be. Resting back into our Awareness and being an observer of the work of our Soul is a sound strategy.

"My Soul sings its Song". When we rest back, we give our Soul the room to do its work. It will move in ways that passes all understanding.

"In this moment I am consciously conscious". This mantra transports me right to that place where I am Pure Awareness.

- **Appreciation.** An internal or external expression of gratitude will shoot our state of mind, our vibrational frequency up in a flash.

"In this moment I appreciate….." (fill in the blank). Taking a moment to appreciate what we have or what we are seeing.

appreciate you for ……" (fill in the blank, be specific). This can be a thought or, better yet, something said to someone who we appreciate. If you say it to someone, be specific if you can, and come from your heart.

"Thank you, Spirit for Life". Spirit is the Source of Life. A "thank you" from time to time is in order.

"Isn't that…(person or thing) amazing?" Yep. They all are.

- **Sacred Senses.** Our physical senses have a spiritual counterpart when we begin to move into 5-Dimensional Awareness. We can see, hear, touch, smell, taste, and breathe sacredly, and alter our perception of your world. There much more to say about Sacred Senses, which I do in my companion book, The Meditation Book (reproduced in an appendix below). Here are a few examples.

"I see your Soul". If there is one key skill to learn in a lifetime, it's the ability to look past the readily apparent, past our judgments, and see the Soul of another. It's right there, waiting for us to notice.

"Amazing Grace how sweet the sound" from the song Amazing Grace. It is interesting that Grace, a gift from Spirit, is described as having a sound, a vibration that can be heard with the Sacred Ear.

"I smell the love in this food". Using our Sacred Sense of smell to come into a moment of Now makes it possible to perceive the love that was cooked into the food.

"The feel of this is exquisite". The texture, temperature, composition elements, and the color of something lovely can knock me out.

• **It's All Sacred.** Here's what I wrote about this in my meditation journal: "This continues to surface as an experience. Sitting in the back yard this evening, with the full moon coming up over the hill, conversing with Lynne, cat purring on my lap, I had a strong feeling of the sacredness of my human experience. Sometimes this 'happening' occurs and it gives me shivers."

"This traffic is a sacred gathering". Life is not all peaches and cream, but it is all sacred. All of it. Including the traffic. Vibe up and enjoy it. See with Sacred Eyes. Listen to something inspiring on your sound system. Sing. Giggle. Fuss gently.

"I see the glow in that…." (object, thing of Nature, person). All things have their 5D counterpart if we can train ourselves to see it. They glow.

"They're really saying I love you" from the song <u>What a Wonderful World</u>, written by Bob Thiele and George David Weiss, and first sung by Louis Armstrong. They penetrate what people "shaking hands, saying 'how do you do'" means--that people are really saying "I love you" to each other. "Oh, yeaaahhhhhh…" (quoting Armstrong's conclusion to the song).

- **Difficult situations**. Difficult situations stimulate our reptilian brain and our fight or flight instincts, whether the "danger" we perceive is physical, emotional, or mental, whether it is real or not. This makes it awfully hard to remember and consider any other alternatives besides the ones that will put us back into our 3d comfort zones.

"I take a Sacred Breath or two and transform this situation". Taking a Sacred Breath can shift our perception of a situation and can shift the situation itself.

"I fear not, for Spirit is with me". When Spirit is with us, there <u>is</u> nothing to fear. The <u>Old Testament</u> Psalmist says, "Yea though I walk through the Valley of the Shadow of Death, I will fear no evil. For Thou art with me."

"That's a Sacred Brother who just cut me off". As mentioned before, a Sacred Breath and a shift in consciousness changes everything.

Ask your Self, **"How can I break this cycle, good buddy?"** Difficult situations are often cyclical. They appear to repeat themselves so that if we can break the underlying cycle, be that karmic or an emotional "stuck place" we are released. Ask the question. Sooner or later the answer will come.

- **Decision making**. We all struggle to make good decisions, especially when they are key decisions with significant consequences. A big part of the problem is the process and criteria we use to make these decisions. Here is the process. First, define the issue as best as you can. Answer these questions: What is the issue? What are the alternatives? What are the impacts of the alternatives on me and others? What feelings do I have related to the alternatives? What have I already tried? What about that worked and didn't work? Then ask for guidance from your Self. Listen. Over several days, if necessary. Make notes of what you "get".

"May this decision reflect my Soul's highest good". This sequence of statements might all be used at a time of big decision, and in this order.

"Self, give me some perspective". Asking for help from our Soul puts us in a state of Spirit/Mind, from which to See and Do. When we ask, we then we have to listen not proscribe or explain or justify.

"What's the right thing to do in this situation for everybody involved?" This question goes beyond what is right for me but for others—for all of us. From the perspective that we are all tied together, One Humanity, each decision does affect everybody else. Changes the dynamic, doesn't it?

"With this decision I plant seeds for Eternity". Decisions imply turning points, choices between alternatives. See the choice as having an Eternal perspective.

In the pursuit of a good decision, we can be assured that if we are aligned with our Higher Selves about a decision and an action, and He is aligned with us, the way is open. Spirit, our HiC, will do most of the work related to action if we will allow It to do so, because that is one of its functions--to help move us along about things needing to be done and done by you specifically. As was said before, "I go before you to make the crooked places straight", the Scriptures promise us.

In some ways all action is sacred, in the same way that all things are sacred. However, some are more "sacred" than others. If the action has a Higher Consciousness component attached to it, something that will uplift you and others, something that raises individual and collective vibration, it is probably worth doing. Let your HiC be your guide. But act. Don't just think or Be and decide that it is enough.

- **Stress**. Upsets, worries about the past or the future. Adrenaline is flowing. Your ego/mind is racing. Your point of attention is misplaced. Shift it with…..

"Peace, be still". As stated earlier, this is one of the most powerful mantras that can be used to deal with lots of situations, especially stressful ones. Many of our concerns, scenarios of outcomes, and consequences never come to pass. This mantra introduces peace into the ego/mind mix and can reign in our wild stallion of a mind.

"I breathe Spirit into this moment". Can't say too often, "Take a Sacred Breath". Let Spirit enter in to change the dynamic of the moment.

"I let go and let Spirit take over". Even more proactively, step back and rest in Spirit.

"I look at this situation with Sacred Eyes". How we "look" at things, the internal filters of the past, fear thought forms, attachment to outcomes, and more, affects how we perceive them and how they turn out. Look with your Soul Senses.

- **Love Relationships**. One of our most confounding human issues, relationships, are complicated. So many forces are at play, yours/mine/ours, and most of us are not particularly good at relating effectively.

"I will become the person I want to attract. A mighty companion." Back to the Law of Attraction, like attracts like; we attract into our relationship world those who vibrate at a similar frequency as we. Poor self-esteem and aggressive behavior are two ends of the same stick for the people involved. If you want to attract a mighty companion to relate to, become that and attract him/her to you.

"I am a Divine Being and insist on being treated as such". We <u>are</u> Divine Beings and <u>do</u> deserve to be treated as such. Anything less denigrates who we are and is a waste of time. Use your time in Eternity wisely.

"I consider your best interest equal to mine and want the same from you". Here's where relating to another well can get particularly good, indeed. When we become best friends and provide for each other a "soft place to fall" we have mastered relationships.

"Using Sacred Eyes, I see his/her Divine Essence". This one has been addressed before in a different context. The ability to see the Divine Essence of another, especially a significant other, is a Soul skill that can alter our reality. Take care, however, that you don't ignore the other three mantras in this group and become involved with someone who doesn't share your intent. Spouses of heinous criminals make this mistake when they say, "He's such a good man. He wouldn't do such a thing."

- **Body/Health.** It has been said that "…without good health you have nothing." While a bit of an exaggeration, feeling poorly does dominate our point of attention when it happens. In the 5th Dimension there is no good health or bad health, there is only divine well-being. That quality has the potential to bend 3d reality and dissolve "bad health", putting the consequences aside. Bad health can turn into good health. Sometimes without any apparent external cause. Here are some sacred sayings that may help.

"I am a Being of Divine Health". Divine Health transcends human health and can influence it. Paralyzed people can be Divinely Healthy, and radiate Light and Love that illumines their world. Recognizing our status of "Divine Being" will raise our vibration and can influence our human health.

"I radiate the experience I have of Divine Health". When we are in a state of Divine Health, we glow, and others recognize it. Not only that, but this is the state that our Master Teachers experienced and from which they were able to influence the physical, mental, emotional, and spiritual health of others around them.

"I Breathe into this...." (injury, prescription drug taking, procedure, or healing process). Taking a Sacred Breath and upping our vibration can positively affect the outcome of these activities. I did this the other day when I cut myself while cooking. Changed the whole experience.

"This body is Spirit's house". Our body is our vehicle for our sojourn on Planet Earth. It's a vehicle which our consciousness occupies. It will dissolve when our consciousness departs. Let it be a temple that Spirit occupies and from which Spirit flows out into our world.

- **Sports/Exercise.** Moving our body skillfully is one of the great pleasures in life. To master a complicated sport like golf, it is said, takes 20,000 hours of practice for which most of us don't have the time. However, it is possible to get into the "Zone", a state of personal high performance, by using some of these:

"I take a Sacred Breath/Sacred Breaths before I...." (serve the tennis ball, lift the weight, dive into the pool). Taking such a breath allow us to activate your Awareness and relax, two things that coaches say are needed to improve performance.

"I take Sacred Breaths <u>while</u> I...." (do tai chi, whiz down the ski slope, run a marathon). This mindfulness exercise can be applied to any activity to help us stay in the moment and enjoy the activity and experience the satisfaction of doing a good job. I used this many times over the past 12 years as I was building my house on the river in Hickory, NC. This, along with idea that if I would take just a few more minutes to correct a mistake, I would satisfy my sense of quality and would do something that would last for 100 years.

Ask any one of these questions when going for a mindfulness walking meditation: **"How slowly can I walk?" "Which toe touches the ground first?" "What is the sound of the grass or gravel on which I am walking?" "What are the birds saying?" "How** warm is the sun on my skin?" Considering these questions turns off the chattering mind and puts us into the role of observer in the moment.

"I <u>let</u> my body hit the ball." Or "I <u>let</u> my serve serve itself". These mantras are inspired by Tim Galway, author of <u>The Inner Game of Tennis</u>, who advocates getting the ego/mind out of the way and letting the body's natural proclivity to perform a task take over. Letting our Soul hit the ball, in effect.

- **Work/Chores.** Most of us spend a significant portion of time earning a living at our profession, as well as traveling to and fro and even working during our free time hours. Getting into the "Zone" at work or at home can be greatly beneficial, especially if we are doing something we love to do. This can be our contribution to the world's economic and spiritual well-being.

"Chop wood, carry water", a mindfulness Zen saying. The full lesson is "before enlightenment, chop wood, carry water; after enlightenment, chop wood carry water". We all have to chop wood and carry water, literally or figuratively, so we might as well do the task mindfully as not.

"Isn't this fun!" It's been interesting to be to use this one for myself. It shifts my mood into a lighter one, especially if I am annoyed or resentful about doing something.

"I infuse this work that I do with a higher vibration". I find that I simply do a better job, and get more satisfaction, if my vibration is higher than lower while I do anything.

"I choose my work based on 'right livelihood.' Right livelihood is a concept that I came across when I was in my late 20s and have followed the precepts of ever since. I decided that since I would be working for many years into the future, I might as well do work that I enjoy, that contributes to the betterment of the world, and with people with whom I enjoy working. This approach has served me well.

- **Abundance.** True wealth, true prosperity, comes with the ability to go Within under any circumstance and access our Higher Consciousness. The ability to do that, and to raise our vibration to a higher level, can be the substance of the ideas, the proper reactions, the resources, the attraction of people and circumstances to our affairs. True wealth, then, the pearl of great price, is our state of elevated awareness and our ability to access that state of awareness anytime it is needed.

"I am abundant in many ways, for which I am thankful". We are all abundant in many ways: physical "stuff", relationships, tree leaves in the fall, pets, entertainment opportunities, etc. Acknowledging this and being grateful for our abundance helps to generate the vibration to attract more.

"Spirit is the Source of my abundance". Once you begin to get over into 5D Reality you realize that Spirit is our Source for everything. Acknowledging that puts the entire abundant Universe at our disposal.

"Yes" to the beggar and give <u>him</u> a "thank you". I almost always carry a few dollars in my pocket. In Vallejo, California, where I live, the town has its share of homeless people and there are a number of folks needing money to exist. I share what I have happily and almost always have a moment of connection during which <u>I</u> get a little lift.

"I am a good steward of my resources". There are lots of things we can do with the resources with which we have been entrusted. Using them consciously and wisely should be considered when we have choices to make about what to do with them.

- **Change.** Internal change, external change; change is a constant. The ego/mind likes sameness, to create a world that is comfortable and safe, and gets nervous about change. These contradictory dynamics cause many people a constant low level of anxiety. Here are some spiritual strategies:

"Change is constant. I welcome this change." Change is the currency of our human experience. Welcoming it and participating in the direction the change takes is a choice that can uplift and provide an opportunity to go beyond our ego/mind boundaries.

"I go Within and embrace this change". Finding a way to bring your consciousness into a situation that is changing can help bring about positive change.

"HiC, let's do this change together". One way to bring consciousness to change is to open up and allow your Soul to participate.

"I choose change in the direction of Spirit". There is almost always a higher vibrational choice at a time of change. Choosing to include that element in the process can be helpful to the outcome.

"I choose to turn this change over to Spirit" is a similar sentiment.

This a long list of options, of "quickie" mindfulness meditations. They cover a lot of the human experience. Consider taking one or two to start with and broaden your repertoire as time goes along.

Questions to Consider
Which two would you start with? Why?

Does this discussion encourage to create your own?

CHAPTER 6

Sacred Speaking

And then there is the speaking, inwardly or outwardly, of these Sacred words and phrases. Twentieth century mystic Alice Baily said some interesting thing about this:

"The basis of all manifested phenomena is the enunciated sound, (words), or the (Sacred) Word spoken with power, with the full purpose of the will behind it.

Words of Power are intended for soul use…..because only the soul can really employ these Words and sounds and thus produce the desired results, which are always in line with the Divine Plan. ….They must be used by the soul in a dynamic manner, involving the serious recognition of the will aspect."

What developing mystics learn to do, she continues, is "make sounds consciously and thus produce a studied and desired result, and be fully aware of the consequences on all planes, and to create forms and direct energy through sacred sounds, and thus further the ends of evolution……To produce results in physical matter, consonant with the clearly defined purpose of the inner God....Every word stirs up the spirit kingdom to help create the forms intended."

My ideas about this:

- Sounds and words generate a cloud of vibration. Sacred Words and the saying of them cause higher vibration which the Universe responds to with Its own sacred response. "Like begets like".
- The use of sounds like Sacred Music sounds can generate a very elevated state in a room. Playing such Music can encourage our own elevation of Awareness into Higher Consciousness. Sacred Sounds/Music can promote healing, as many who know about such things will attest. Steven Halpern is one of a number of people who have developed such Music.
- Feelings and thoughts create words, words create belief and intent, belief and intent create action--all of which is influenced by the vibration of each. Words, therefore, are loaded with meaning and vibration. It is important to not use idle words, negative thoughts and words, and words congruent with less desirable, rather than more desirable outcomes. The further we advance in this work the more important it is to consider the impact on ourselves and our Universe of our thoughts and words. Alice Bailey suggests that we be mindful that we want to "produce results in physical matter, consonant with the clearly defined purpose of the inner God."
- Words, likewise, can help generate elevated awareness and promote healing. Especially, as Alice Baily is saying, when the Sacred Words are used by the Soul in a dynamic manner to further the ends of evolution. The best example I have of this is Jesus saying, "Peace, be

still" to the storm that had overtaken the boat he was traveling in and the storm stopped. These were Sacred Words coming out of the mouth of one of our Master Teachers and you know they had Intent and Soul and Power.

- There are very few of us who have a sufficiently strong consciousness to quieten a storm. However, in the end, it is the movement of Spirit, from within, from Soul, that can alter 3d reality, not the power of the individual speaking the words, silently or aloud. It is Spirit that elevates a 3d situation into a 5D situation.

- We all can do this if we learn to quieten down enough, to get in touch with the Kingdom that lies Within, to generate enough of a sense of Awareness of our own Eternal Beingness, to have Spirit move out from us into 3d reality and alter the direction of things, if only a minute amount. And, like any muscle exercised, the more we do such things the better we get at it. Especially by getting very familiar with the Soul part of ourselves, our Higher Consciousness, by any means possible. The best way, from my experience, is through meditation. Especially Higher Consciousness Meditation.

- My inclination is to concentrate on the development of my own Christ Consciousness, and that everything will follow in due course (one of the central themes of my next book on the subject, Book 4, on the subject of the Laws of Vibration and Abundance.) As well as to surround myself with Sacred Sounds. And to use words very carefully because they do create things.

- It takes going Within and touching that Soul part of us, I think, to know what the Highest Expression of Spirit is.

By doing so Spirit is released. "Breathe Me and I/Spirit will go forth" my HiC said to me. Don't beg or insist that something happen--that's just human mind getting involved. Let Spirit go forth and do Its work. We are merely openings through which Spirit can enter 3d reality and have that reality be influenced by 5D Reality. And watch. Behold. Nothing obvious may happen. That is not the point. It's not your concern. It is the touching of our Withiness that is the important thing to have occur. Let the results be what they are meant to be.

Questions to Consider

Does your spiritual tradition use prayer? To influence events or gain some benefit over another? After this discussion, have you changed your mind about praying this way? How?

CHAPTER 7

Mudra Meditations

A mudra is a body or hand position that creates divine or uplifting vibrations. Some Eastern traditions make extensive use of a variety of mudras, each having a different energetic effect on our body and our awareness by their use. They are not foreign to the West, however, although they are not called mudras, per se. Witness the hand over the heart with the two-finger wiggle that Kevin Costner's character and his granddaughter used in the movie <u>Black and White</u> to signal "I love you" to each other. Or the two finger "V for Victory" gesture made famous by Winston Churchill, which helped to energize the British people during World War II.

These gestures can be done quickly and very unobtrusively to elevate our state of awareness. As kinetic movements they have a different effect on the body's vibration from words said silently or aloud, yet they can be combined with words or phrases to heighten the intended effect.

Below are a few that I like. If you want to explore this further go to the internet and type in "mudras and love", for example, and you will find a number of gestures that have been used to represent and generate that feeling. Typing in "therapeutic mudras" or "mudra for headache" will direct you to gestures that are said to be able to address a migraine and other specific physical ailments. My intention in introducing this concept, as with other techniques presented in this book, is to give you a tool to elevate your Awareness and raise your vibration.

Jesus of Nazareth is often depicted standing with his right hand raised and his left hand over his heart. His raised right hand is said to be a gesture of "fear not" and the left a gesture of love. A similar gesture with our right hand reminds us that there is nothing to be afraid of. For a moment of experiencing love simply place your hand over your heart and breathe.

The Gyan Mudra, shown below, is one of the most recognized mudras used by Hindus and Buddhists (see illustration 1.a.). It's often used in meditation but is not limited to that use, by any means. With it the index finger and thumb are lightly touching at the tips. The other three fingers are extended in a relaxed manner.

I like to use the Gyan Mudra when I do a 5-minute Higher Consciousness Meditation. It has a calming effect and traditionally, it also inspires creativity, increases concentration, and stimulates the brain, pituitary gland, and endocrine system. There are other times that I do it when I am sitting and chatting or when writing and in need of a creative thought.

Shuni Mudra (1.b.) promotes patience, courage, and noble thoughts, as well as transforms negative emotions into positive ones. It also represents stability, strength, and perseverance.

1.a   1.b   1.c

Surya Ravi Mudra (1.c.) promotes energy, positivity, and intuition. It helps to build and invigorate the bodily tissues. It is also known for speeding up the metabolism and energizing the whole body.

This configuration of the hands, in the lap while sitting cross legged, is one of the most common mudras for meditating; It can also be done with the fingers interlaced, the right thumb on top.

This combination of right hand pointed/touching the earth and the left resting in the lap is the one that Gautama Buddha was using when he became enlightened. The right hand was touching the earth, grounding him, and protecting him from the temptations of the mind.

FUGEN BOSATSU

This is a mudra of greeting, respect, and veneration. A symbolic gesture of reverence, it symbolizes the unity of body and mind.

This is the arrangement of hands is often used when greeting someone with the salutation 'Namaste", translated as "The Soul in me greets the Soul in You."

It's also a symbol of reverence and has become widely use in the age of the Covid19 virus as an alternative to shaking hands.

Questions to Consider

Does the use of mudras, hand gestures, interest you? Why?

CHAPTER 8

Some Other "Quickies"

Here are a few more "quickies" for specific purposes:

• Take a moment as soon as you wake up, before getting up, appreciate the day. Say to yourself, "I am an Eternal Being. I am Eternal Beingness." Do the same when you pull up the covers up at night to go to sleep.

• Pause as you go out of your front door to take a Sacred Breath and raise your vibration as you make that transition. We go in and out of doors frequently. The idea is to make an association between one activity (passing through a door) and another (taking a Sacred Breath).

Observant Jews take this practice one step further. Inside a little rectangular case, mounted on the door frame, is kept a Mezuzah--two chapters from the Torah written on a rolled-up parchment. The first verse is "Hear oh Israel, the L-rd is our G-d, the L-rd is One." When leaving the house, they touch the Mezuzah and remember that God is One. We can borrow from this tradition and put whatever we want on the door frame to touch as a reminder to elevate our consciousness.

• Put a post-it note on your computer screen. Use any of the mindfulness exercises mention earlier in the book. Move it around on the screen from time to time as needed because it can get in the way of seeing the screen's text. Also, refresh the color of the post it or change the phrase occasionally. The post-it tends to "disappear" from view, otherwise, although they are right there on your screen.

• One of my favorite triggers is the wooden jute beads that I often wear on my wrist. They are light, unobtrusive and have a nice feel to them. Here's what I wrote about them a week after starting to use them. "The beads, the beads, pay attention to the beads. When they click, think of HiC. When they slip down on your wrist, think of HiC. Get in the habit of touching them to think of HiC. I'm just looking for a little reminder. Accompany the activity with a little smile. Crinkle the eyes (a good way to "fuzz" out your view for a moment). Be joyful in the remembrance."

• Wear a rubber band on your wrist. The purpose is the same as the beads, to use a physical object to condition you to do or remember something. In my experience, the beads become "old hat" after a while, and I begin to forget them. Exchange them for a rubber band. When I notice the band, if there is no one around, I will "plop" it as a physical reminder to go Within.

• Wear a watch that emits a little beep at the top of every hour for a reminder.

Also take a look at the Sacred Senses in the Addendum below for some more "quickies".

CHAPTER 9.

Conclusion: How and Why

This book has offered a number of tools, mindfulness techniques, to deal with a variety of life's problems and issues that come along. Some address what's going on in the now to help us more effectively deal with the situation right in front of us. Others are intended to simply lift our state of consciousness, our awareness, from human awareness to Higher Consciousness.

It helps to step back from the micro level of a specific problem or individual moment and remember that we have tools to use to bring Awareness to bear on the problem moment. And then choosing a tool or a saying that enables us to bring our Higher Self, our Soul, into the moment. Perhaps helping us remember to be more of who we are, Eternal Beings, not reactive humans.

Each mindfulness technique mentioned above has similar intent. An intent to sift consciousness from everyday reality to spiritual reality. The Spiritual Reality that is inside of us. That *"Kingdom of God (that) is within you"* that Jesus spoke of. We just have to remember to access That Kingdom. By recalling words or phrases, using mindfulness exercises that are triggers, often causes paths to Higher Consciousness open.

Take the phrase "I breathe Spirit into this moment". Something may have happened, and you want to collect yourself, and up your vibratory rate to bring the resources that your Self, your Soul can bring to the moment. Or you just want to pause in the midst of your busy day to enjoy the moment, smell the roses. "I breathe Spirit into this moment" is a good mindfulness technique for either of these situations.

The intent is there, the words come, the shift happens, and we are transported into an Alternate Reality, almost, a Reality that exists within everyday reality where we recognize the sacredness of the moment. And the truth of the phrase "Be Here Now" is recognized--that "Now" is the only moment that there is, that there ever will be, and that it is infused with Spirit, The ALL, Omnipresence, God.

After trying out some of these techniques you will find some that are particularly appealing, for specific situations that you find yourself in frequently. Or for just shifting your consciousness the moment just for the pleasure of it. The more you use a few of these, or maybe just one of them for a while, you may find yourself changing the words to suit yourself or developing one that is your own creation.

That's the How and the Why. A Few More Things to Say

A few more things to say about this subject:
- One of the lovely outcomes of experiencing the State of Peace reached when we say to ourselves, "Peace, Be

Still" is that we can slip into that State of Mind and recognize that we <u>are</u> Eternal Beings.

- It's even possible to have the experience of Eternal Beingness in which we simply Are the Spirit out of which Life flows. One with The ALL. In which we are both the typist and the keyboard, the thought and the observer of the thought emerging from the unfolding of the Universe.

- There is nothing to fear because harmony is the fundamental state of the Universe which unfolds moment by moment, with no harm to anything. Fear and harm are not a vibratory rate in 5-Dimensional Reality. Nothing can harm Omnipresence.

- Such a realization, such an experience, is the ultimate "Why" of working with mindfulness mediation techniques which results in Higher Consciousness. The momentary evaporation of the ego and the illumination of our Consciousness that is connected with Everything, Everywhere, Always.

- This may sound a bit strange because I am trying to talk about the concept and the experience with words so inadequate for the task. But it's the experience spoken of by all of our Master Teachers. And for which we hold them in great reverence. Because they were able to advance to that level of experience and then share it with us.

- They were merely trying to share what they saw and felt in their highest states of Being using the words of their day. With the hope that we too might catch the fire in the words that doesn't burn, but it Illumines. And meditation was one of the ways to "get There" for them and still is for us. Mindfulness meditation can take us there in a flash of realization if we are most fortunate to Be, Here.

- It is most fortunate if we can get to the Place where are living out from the Spirit Within. Letting It be our primary locus of focus and unfolding Life from our Higher Consciousness rather that struggling with life from our human consciousness.

Give these meditation techniques a try and see what you experience. It may take you a while, and a number of tries, until they begin to "take". A while before doing them such that a "release" begins to happen, indicating Spirit is engaged. These techniques are not necessarily used in just this say by most meditation researchers use. Researchers mostly use a simple mindfulness meditation exercise in their studies. I have found, however, that the techniques mentioned above have an additional potency and are worth trying.

A Poem

Sometimes these ideas are best expressed in the language of poetry. Here's one that does a pretty good job.

Spirit Flows, Poem 59

In a nano, Spirit flows.
Flows in, and around, from my Being.
Grace dawns; my Being Be's.
Sometimes a burst, sometimes a stealth.
Always available when I turn Its Way.

Inward.
The path leads…
Inward,
To my holiest of holies,
Inward.
Sacred Senses, heightened,
Detect its Presence.

Infinity at the ready.
My meekest move.
My smallest opening.
My strongest non-wish.
Allow the tsunami to flow.
No-thought will do it.
As will a breath,

Sacred in its intent.

Bliss's too mild for its effect,
Word can't grab the stun of its arrival.
"Arrival" is paltry,
As is "Grace", and "Presence".
Three come to mind.
They pale to mind's inability.
To wrap itself
'Round the experience.

Like wild mushrooms.
Invisible to the unskilled.
'Til consciousness reaches
In and out; eyes ready to see.
Ears perked to hear.
Senses ready, ready for the Beloved.
Primed for the stirring of the Known.
Unknown to the mind which knows It not.
No matter how subtle the thoughts,
A tool that does not work.
A driver without a screw.

Available to the Seeker
Who goes Within,
Quietens the rush,
Opens the heart.
Shifts the view to Isness,
To Beingness,
To Life.

It's Me, It's Thee.

It's everywhere, but no "place",
It's everything, but no "thing",
Words fail. Release.
Thoughtless instant,
Extended breath.
Lifetime search.
Wordless Word,
Jewel's right there.
In Sacred Sight.

CHAPTER 10

Next Steps

My best wishes for your growth and evolution in Higher Consciousness. If you found this book helpful and you want to engage in personal growth and expansion of your awareness, take advantage of the resources that **our website**, HiCMeditation.com provides.

Studies have shown that if an adult wants to learn something s/he will do so more thoroughly and quickly if s/he uses a variety of learning techniques, each of which supports the other. Go to the site HiCMeditation.com for lots to see and do--a blog, articles, sample chapters, poems, and "Healthy Home" product pages.

Our website includes over 100 products we have personally found to be helpful in promoting well-being and encouraging a Healthy Home.

Namaste (The ALL in me acknowledges The ALL in you).

Blessings,

Blair

If you got value from this book please, please, please go to the Kindle Review area and review this book. Many people do not know that a review, even a short one, is like gold to an author. Exposure by Kindle Books, Google rankings and additional book sales are strongly driven by insightful reviews. Thank you!

Addendum A.

Sacred Senses

I wrote about Sacred Senses in Book 2 <u>The Meditation Book</u> and decided that, because they are very much mindfulness exercises, to include that discussion as an addendum to this book. If you've already read Book 2, ignore these.

Sacred Senses are a higher consciousness form of our physical senses and can be used to help us achieve a state of Elevated Awareness, and increase our vibration, if only for a moment. The sacred use of our physical senses to elevate our state of consciousness can be done quickly, can enliven our day, and can propel us into a more illumined state of personal awareness.

The key to taking advantage of our Sacred Senses is remembering to remember to use them. While this may sound odd; it is not. The elevated state of awareness that we experience in Higher Consciousness Meditation is incredibly attractive. It is really our true state of being. I would love to be in this state all the time. I'm happier, sharper, more intuitive, and more fun to be with when I am more conscious.

However, my state of Higher Consciousness achieved during meditation inevitably "wears off" as my morning unfolds. Sometimes something catches my attention and pulls me into its "realm", its vibration. If I have to get out on the freeway, the demands of that activity are very compelling and I forget my elevated state as my normal, everyday 3d consciousness takes over and drives me to my destination.

Fortunately, I now know that I have another option, but I have to remember to remember to exercise that set of muscles. Like any new skill, it has to be used. Like any new set of learnings, it takes a while to master them and have them become our "new normal". Developing and using our Sacred Senses can help elevate consciousness and is intrinsically rewarding just in the doing.

Also, keep in mind that each of us prefers the use of the 5 senses in normal, everyday life. Some people are more visually oriented and will say "I see what you are saying" instead of "I hear what you are saying", revealing a personal sense preference for seeing rather than hearing. Consider your personal preference and "see" if you like some or one of the Sacred Senses more than the others.

Some of the examples offered below are meditative practices and some are mindfulness practices, as you will see in the methods and examples presented. Meditation and mindfulness practices are often two sides of the same coin.

Sacred Seeing

Sacred Seeing is one of the most powerful ways we can use to elevate our consciousness. Sacred Seeing involves more than the typical way to see by taking in and processing visual information. Shifting into a higher state of awareness with seeing can be done in these ways:

- See the Soul, or Higher Self in others. This is a big one for me, so I will spend some extra time on it. My 3d mind has a strong proclivity to be judge, jury and executioner. Not so very long ago I slowed down long enough to recognize how pervasive is my need, desire, compulsion to judge everyone I meet. I still catch my body/mind/personality making up stories about everything I see. "That car means this person is well-to-do, a go-getter." "That old Pontiac Lemans means that person is only able to afford an old car with dents. He "should" fix those dents" ("should" is a word my body/mind/personality uses quite a bit). "That person looks like someone who doesn't care about his health, has no discipline to keep himself fit, and should do something about it."

- Crazy stuff--stuff swimming around at such a low level of consciousness that it's embarrassing to acknowledge the truth of it. At least now, however, I have slowed down enough to notice what kinds of thoughts are flowing through my brain, and to look Within to ask "Well, what is that all about?" Of course, the answer is, "3d mind at work". The 3d mind is a judging mind, a discriminating mind, a justifying mind, a mind that makes things up when faced with a lack of information. Well, that's not exactly right. In reality, my mind makes things up all of the time. Rain or shine. It makes others "wrong" to make myself and my ways "right" --neuron firings to justify my behavior and the quirks of my personality.

- Sacred Seeing is the blessed antidote to mental judgment. I have been practicing with Lynne as we sit in the evening, having a glass of wine and debriefing the day. I see her in all of her magnificence, and it moves me. My vibration shoots up.

- I also practice Sacred Seeing when I go to the grocery store. **Here's the technique: Take a Sacred Breath. Squint a little and soften your eyes. Look to see if you can see the Christ in those around you. Even for just a flash.**

  It works. When I am successful, my mind shifts up to the 5th Dimension and I can see people's auras. I see them from a loving perspective, am in a gentle state, acknowledge them with a smile, and the whole store seems to light up.

- Sacred Seeing allows us to take in more, relevant, intuitive information about something of which we might not, otherwise, be aware. For example, I can look at a plant outside of the house with Sacred Eyes and see its state of health—its need for water, its need for sunshine, whether its location is favorable, or it needs to be moved. Lynne has taught me this with her power of non-judgmental seeing, one of her strengths about people and things.

Using this one technique, alone, could cause anyone to become illumined in this lifetime, if we can perfect it and "see" all things and people around us this way.

This evening, for example, I was petting our beloved Annie Cat. All at once, I shifted into a different valence of "seeing", and "saw" that I was petting myself. That I was not body limited but had shifted into seeing my immediate surroundings as "me" and my Oneness with It (my surroundings). This is what true compassion must be, a sense of Oneness in which all is well, and all is beloved, and the object of my attention is Sacred.

Sacred Tasting/Smelling/Eating

If you're like me, you tend to eat too fast and don't enjoy your food enough. Sacred Tasting (and Smelling) is so important to the enjoyment, consumption, and processing of food.

- I first became aware of the notion of Sacred Tasting at the Integral Yoga Institute in San Francisco in 1975. Lynne and I took a vegetarian cooking class there on Saturday mornings for several months. The class would prepare lunch for ourselves and for the staff, about 15 people.

  We ate together in silence, the first time I had ever heard of doing such a thing. Called mindful eating, the practice was done in silence and we were to take one bite, put down our fork, and chew until the last swallow before taking another bite. It took a while longer than usual to eat, granted, but I learned to savor the food, pay attention to its smells, distinguish various spices, notice the texture of the ingredients, and eat peacefully.

- Over the years I had abandoned the practice of paying that type of attention to my food until recently. With my deepening meditation practice and with Lynne's urging, I am relearning not to bolt down my food and pay more attention, to be more aware, of the loveliness of what I am eating.

- In my research I have found nutritionists say that this technique helps people to lose weight. This makes sense to me as I am much more aware of when I have had an "ample sufficiency", as my father-in-law used to say, and thereby avoid eating too much because of the inertia of eating too fast. I also think that I sometimes have engaged in "emotional eating" --taking in too much food when I am emotionally agitated. Mindful eating can help with this tendency, as well.

- The Zen Buddhist teacher, Thich Nat Hahn, speaks this way of drinking tea, which also applies to eating and any other mindfulness practice, "Drink your tea slowly and reverently, as if it is the axis on which the world earth revolves--slowly, evenly, without rushing toward the future. Live the actual moment. Only this moment is life."

- Our vegetarian cooking class also introduced us to the idea that being in a peaceful state of mind is important for the cook. Not only did we eat in silence, but we also prepared the food in respectful silence as well. Our teacher, Swami Nirmalananda, more than once reminded us of the importance of not being agitated or upset when we were in the kitchen. (Lynne and I were in a difficult time in our relationship and sometimes we would bring that energy to the Saturday morning class.) She said that if we were upset, we would cook that into the food and give our diners indigestion. She was a saint to put up with us the way she did. Thanks Swami. We made it!

- Lastly, Lynne and I have become more and more conscious over the years about the quality and type of food we eat. We go to the farmer's market as much as possible to get organic fruit and vegetables, and organic meats at the grocery story. Our typical evening meal is an entrée and a salad, sometimes with frozen yogurt to top it off.

Recently we began experimenting with a style of cooking called Ayurveda. It's an ancient Hindu practice based on several ideas:

- The way food is prepared can be healing in nature as well as healthy. The courses, the ingredients, and the spices can be selected in such a way as to promote overall health as well as to target particular health conditions so as to promote the healing of those conditions. We have been using The Ayurveda Cookbook by Amadea Morningstar, which also talks quite a bit about the philosophy behind the practice.

We won't use this system exclusively; we may use the recipes once or twice a week. Conceptually, the approach makes sense, though. We have also experimented with putting chicken or shrimp in her recipes as we are not vegetarians. This has worked quite well.

- Ayurveda also uses the Hindu concept of personality types and the importance of matching up the type of food and ingredients to your personality type. (There's a little profile quiz to determine your personality type if you want to pursue this idea at https://www.theayurvedaexperience.com/dosha-quiz/). People, like the two of us, who are "Pita" types (tending toward being fiery, strong willed and determined) should avoid fried foods, caffeine and hot spices, for example, and emphasize fresh fruit, vegetables, milk products and whole grains.

Sacred Touching

There are a number of practices that we can undertake to touch with exquisiteness. There's nothing like the feel of a baby's skin, snow, alpaca fabric, the seams of a baseball, bird feathers, a heating pad, soft lips, and more. Being mindful of the feel of the world around us helps bring us into the "here and now" --to be more present and possibly to feel the Presence of Spirit.

It's possible to enjoy all types of touch sensations when we slow down to pay attention to this sense: texture, hardness, temperature, roughness, aliveness, cleanliness, and more.

- I was recently introduced to the idea of using touch as a way of short-circuiting thought by an on-line tennis teacher, Will Hamilton. (I use tennis analogies throughout my writing because I play and because I am applying these principals to playing better and with more enjoyment.) In tennis and golf, it is important to stay calm and relaxed to play well, unlike football where an adrenaline rush can help you tackle harder.

However, when at the end of a set of tennis and I am serving to win the set, it is amazingly easy for my mind to imagine the consequences of winning or blowing it, choking, and cause the adrenaline to begin to flow— sometimes dramatically. The result is that I sometimes tighten up, lose the flow of my serve, and may end up hitting the ball into the net.

Will has a friend who is sports psychologist and fellow teacher who says that the best thing that we can do in that moment is the following:

- Walk around a bit and feel the ground with your feet
- Bounce the ball three times and watch it bounce. Feel the fuzz on the ball.
- Breathe in through the nose and out through the mouth.
- Feel the texture of the racquet handle. Loosen your grip on the racquet.
- Watch the seams of the ball rotate as you toss the ball upwards.
- Extend your arm and keep it up there an extra second instant to stay more upright.

He maintains that doing these things causes the mind to quieten, since the brain can't process both thought and feeling at the same time. Concentrating on touch shorts out the thoughts and the emotional flow of unwanted adrenaline. Not only do I find that these things work but they are lessons for daily life.

If we are about to get up and give a speech, which most people hate, it can help to take an object from your pocket, perhaps a special stone, and focus on the texture and feel of it. Become aware of the feel of your feet on the floor as you walk to the podium. Touch the podium with interest and feel the texture of the top of it.

There are all kinds of situations to which we can apply this technique when staying calm is the order of the day.

Sacred Hearing

"Do you hear what I am saying?" is a common plaintive cry of one human to another. While, on one hand, it is impossible to really and truly know fully and completely what another is saying or feeling, we all want to be heard and understood by the important people in our lives. Sacred Hearing or Listening can bridge that gap.

Really "hearing" somebody is an art. Not being "heard" can be excruciatingly frustrating. In my business consulting work at the SBTDC in North Carolina I spent considerable time training our consultants, especially the new ones, to be good, active listeners. This key skill is one few newbies had when they began working with us. Mirroring back to the client what he or she might have just said was helpful. As was rephrasing their commentary and asking if that is what was meant often clarified an issue. Asking the client to "tell me more about that" helped to drill down into a problem to get at the root cause. It helped us to help clients discover their own answers to problems and issues they were having if I was listening to them intently.

- One key technique that is often used in mindfulness workshops is Sacred Walking--walking slowly and observing as much as possible of what is going within us, and around us, in the process of walking our bodies. The instructions often include "open your Inner Ear" to hear the symphony of sounds of nature cascading around you.

- Listening to our inner voice, our intuition, or our individual Higher Consciousness, the HiC that I spoke of earlier, is an example of Sacred Listening and Hearing. It has been said that the best form of prayer is one of listening rather than speaking. Offering gratitude for Divinity's gifts rather asking Divinity for more, more, more, as if God were a Santa Claus, can also open those Sacred Ears.

- Sacred music has a higher vibratory rate. Some music is known to have healing properties, including "soothing the savage beast". See the topic "Sacred Music" below.

Sacred Healing

While healing is not necessarily one of the five senses, I would certainly put Healing into the category of Sacred Senses. I will be brief in my remarks about healing in this book and will have much more to say about that in a future volume.

We all have been wounded physically, emotionally, mentally, and spiritually. Some have been severely wounded in one or more of these areas. It's part of the human condition that I mentioned earlier, part of the landscape of a material world. If we fall, we skin our knees. Someone screaming at us can leave an emotional scar. Severe traumas can affect us for a whole lifetime if they are not dealt with effectively.

Higher Consciousness Meditation can be helpful to the healing process in a number of ways. First, being in a state of Higher Consciousness generates a higher physical, mental, emotional, spiritual vibration. Higher vibrations tend to ward off illness and to mitigate the frequency and severity of a state of a dis-ease. Many physical conditions are caused by fear and a high-octane lifestyle.

A higher state of vibration can augment the healing properties of a medical procedure or cause a dis-ease to begin to melt away in the sunlight of Spirit. Also, those who are in a state of Higher Consciousness tend to make better choices about their habits and routines, and make choices to avoid lower level vibrational, less healthy activities.

Most of our Master Teachers were said to be superb healers. Spontaneous healings often occurred to those with various afflictions from just being in their presences. I think this occurred because the atmosphere around them was so charged with higher vibration that dis-eases just melted in the presence of the Teacher's Illumination. Healing benefits are available to those who case raise their internal vibrations through practices like Higher Consciousness Meditation.

As I mentioned earlier, healing will be the in-depth subject of another book, but I would like to mention one use of Sacred Breathing that I have used recently in certain situations where healing was called for. For example, I have found that if I cut my face shaving, strain a muscle, or bang myself somehow, and I remember to take a mental step back from the trauma of what has just happened to take a Sacred Breath, two things occur. First, I calm myself down more quickly to assess and react better to the situation, and second, the healing process seems to take less time. I think the latter is true because my body goes into a higher state of vibration immediately before the trauma takes over, and that promotes accelerated recovery.

Questions to Consider

Like the idea of Sacred Senses? Which one is most attractive to you? Why?

What problem/issue/concern would you like to apply your Sacred Senses to?

Another Poem

Vibration, All is Vibration

From time to time, I am moved to write a poem. This one seems particularly apropos to the subject of mindfulness and of observing the vibration of all things.

One morning, as I concluded my yoga practice, I was struck by the experience that everything seemed to slow down, and, furthermore, that everything is in vibration. I stopped and jotted down the following, "All is moving and still at the same time. This creates an interesting tension, the interval between one wave and another. It's here that Lifeforce happens. Set in motion by the Big Bang, set in motion by a rustling, a stirring. I felt a poem coming on."

Genesis

Rustling, rustling, stirring.
An eyelid opens,
Consciousness stirs
Within the ALL.

Lazy quarks sway to and fro, bestirring themselves,
Ready for another adventure of expanding out and out and out.
Gravity emerges
And swirls the stew of eternity, of infinity.
Thought is born and shoots out,
Looking for a response.
The stirring of another thought on the other side of eternity,
infinity—two/one.
And I yawn.
What shall this new One bring?

ABOUT THE AUTHOR

This book is one in a series of books that I am writing based on my study of spiritual matters over the past 40+ years and the application of principals that I have learned in my life. (My Story appears in other books, as well.)

As I began to write about my author bio, I realized that I had two stories tell. One was the three-dimensional version: I was born, I have lived, and I will die someday. The other is a 5-

Dimensional version that chronicles the relative brief period of the life of an Eternal Being in the latter part of the 20th and the early part of the 21st Centuries.

Version One

- Russell "Blair" Abee, Jr. was born in a 3-dimensional reality on Planet Earth in the middle of the 20th Century. I'm a "baby boomer" and write books. That's it. Someday, I'll go to heaven, hell, or oblivion.
- I was born to parents in North Carolina who seemed to love each other and loved me a bunch. I have three younger brothers and one sister. I didn't seem to have a lot in common with some in this group, but the DNA is strong.
- We went to the Lutheran Church in my youth and believed in Jesus as the only Son of God. I bought it all.
- I went to school, lots of it. In undergraduate school I became an atheist because I concluded that the Jesus story was a fairy tale.
- Graduated. Moved to San Francisco.
- My BA in Political Science and a quarter bought me a cup of coffee in the world of work. Started a business remodeling old Victorian houses to survive and stay in California.
- Went back to school to get a master's degree.
- Met a girl. Got married, had 2 kids, boys, and now, 3 grandchildren, boys.
- Had friends, and a few people I disliked.
- Had different jobs. Owned some businesses. Went into government service as a business consultant.

- Retired after 20 years.
- Will die sometime in the next 30 years.
- Most of my world and its activities seem random, with some interesting coincidences along the way.
- My world is a world of duality—black/ white, good/bad; love/hate, hopes/fears

Version Two

- I, Blair Abee, was born in a 5-Dimensional Reality on planet Earth, in what may be one of many Intelligent Universes. I reincarnated in the middle of the 20th Century after many lifetimes stretching back to the beginning of this Universe and will never "die". That is, my consciousness will never be lost.
- I have a purpose, an Eternity Purpose, which is to grow and develop into my destiny as a Universal Citizen. I am learning to live a Spirit guided life to fulfill my Purpose.
- I chose my parents after considering our past lives together, the karma that was in play as a result of our previous associations, and the possibility that I may be able to fulfill my Purpose this lifetime, or significantly move myself along the Path. In the process, I would be able to erase much of the karma that I had accumulated with my two life sponsors.
- My childhood and educational career were much the same as described above.
- I moved to San Francisco, California, and started on my spiritual Path and began to work in earnest on my Purpose.
- I began with a Jungian dream workshop and spent many years exploring the self-help arena.

- I started doing yoga 43 years ago and began my exploration of Zen Buddhism.

- Met my wife Lynn at a "Be Here Now" workshop and we had an immediate connection/recognition. During our long, somewhat contentious courtship, we burned off a lot of personal and couple karma. It became clearer and clearer that we had a Soul connection, companions in many lifetimes, and compatible on many levels. We married.

- We have two children, Ivan (my stepson and good friend) and Justin (our son together). They chose us and we chose them—Ivan needed two dads. They are mighty companions.

- We have had a variety of friends and relatives with whom we have clearly spent lifetimes and generated karma. Some are members of our Soul Group.

- I was strongly influenced by the Buddhist concept of "right livelihood" in my career choices and have managed to live by this principal of doing good work, with compatible, enjoyable people, for most of my work career.

- In the past couple of years, I have found myself really "waking up" and becoming deeply involved in meditation. This has resulted in developing my own form of meditation, Higher Consciousness Meditation. Consequently, I have come to know my Soul, my individual Higher Consciousness, and have come to many of the realizations expressed in this book. Most importantly, I have come to experience the idea that we all have within us a Higher Consciousness, the same one fully expressed by Krishna, Jesus, and Buddha, among others.

- I have come to realize that I exist in a 5-Dimensional Universe of infinite complexity, much of which I know nothing about, consciously.

- I am working on my Purpose and being led by Spirit, mostly but not totally, represented by my Higher Consciousness, which I affectionately call "HiC".

- I know that my physical body will die, that my consciousness, in my Spirit Body, will be elevated into the realm of the Other Side, and that I will continue my Eternity Career there, learning and growing. More than likely I will come back to Earth, with learnings I have gleaned in this lifetime, and will continue the pursuit of my Purpose when I return.

Recent History—The Deep Dive

In many ways, the impetus to write these books was born out of adversity and the need to dive deep into Spirit in order to deal with that adversity.

My trial by fire and my deep dive into Higher Consciousness began in earnest in early 2012 when I took a big promotion and moved to San Diego to become Associate Director of the San Diego Small Business Development Center (SBDC) Network. I had worked in the SBDC system, sponsored by the US Small Business Administration, for 19 years in North Carolina. I was exceptionally good at my profession and worked my way up through the ranks with great success. San Diego was my next stop to the top of my profession, State Director of a SBDC program, somewhere.

Unfortunately, I walked into a professional hell when I moved to San Diego. The Network was being managed by a poor leader and manager. She had been running the program into the ground for over 10 years, abusing employees, manipulating money, and confusing her lackadaisical overseers with a smoke and mirrors game of monumentally devious proportions. Program performance was abysmal. I tried to find out what was going on with the program before I accepted the job, but nobody would tell me the truth. And Lynne and I were anxious to get back to California, after being away for 20 years. Both of our boys lived on the West Coast.

For more than 6 months I tried to learn my new, complex job, and to bring my experience to bear on the situation to improve things. I knew what needed to be done, from previous experience in leading an organizational turnaround, but my ideas were rejected. I ended up in a pitch battle with my supervisor over survival of the program. She began to blame me for all of the problems with the program and she threatened to have me fired as a way of diverting attention from <u>her</u> incompetence.

I blew the whistle, revealing to community college officials who were supposed to be monitoring the program, what was going on. Thus, ensued another 6-month period in which an investigation was done, she got demoted, I was fired, and she was eventually put on indefinite leave. At the time of this writing, the program continued to flounder under new leadership at the corrupt, dysfunctional community college that was our host. Now they are in good hands with a capable leader.

The next 12 months were difficult for me, as well. For 9 of them I tried to find a suitable job in my profession. I came remarkably close to becoming a State Director, being in the final group of two candidates twice, with no success. The same thing happened with Associate State Director and Center Director positions in California and elsewhere. Each time I came up empty handed after traveling quite a bit and interviewing a lot. I'm sure it didn't help that potential employers would contact my former employer and hear.... who knows what?

I also filed a whistle blower action with the California State Personnel Board but lost after a hearing in which college officials accused me of incompetence and lied about various facts in the case. They were willing to stoop to any low, it seemed, to keep from compensating me for their injustices.

Throughout this whole episode, my meditation practice was one of my key anchors to maintaining a sense of well-being. It enabled me to "keep my head while others were losing theirs" (Gunga Din, by Rudyard Kipling). I was able to return over and over again to a reasonably peaceful state of mind, no matter what insanity was going on around me. I managed to stay "in the moment", most of the time. I also started writing about my experiences, with no thought for publishing, but as part of my healing.

I went deeper and deeper into my meditation practice and began to have amazing insights and experiences, including experiences of illumination. And of developing a relationship with my Soul, my Higher Consciousness.

The idea that has been taught by the world's Master Teachers for centuries of Spirit being Within us, and that all we have to do is turn Within for It to come flooding to meet us, began to make a lot of sense to me. In my case, I think my Higher Consciousness has waited many lifetimes, many lifetimes, for me to begin to Awaken and has been such a great, and patient, teacher.

This saga began to remind me of the "Hero's Journey" that Joseph Campbell speaks so eloquently of in his book <u>Hero with A Thousand Faces</u>. In the book he shows that many successful new and old stories follow the same storyline development. The archetypical journey begins, inevitably, with the reluctant hero launching off into a new reality (San Diego for me); having difficult, life altering adventures; discovering treasure in a far-off land; and bringing the treasure or important information back to ordinary reality to share with the village he left.

In my case, I have done a very deep dive into my inner self and have discovered the gold of Higher Consciousness. I have returned to share what I have learned with the village, so we can all celebrate in our good fortune of what I have discovered. I now see the bigger picture of the whys and wherefores of my Journey and have found that I am exactly where I was led to be and doing exactly what I should be doing--sitting here writing this saga.

Added Thoughts

Breathe Me

Another form of meditation. A technique to be used to help take you to the next level. "Breathe me", I say to HiC. Breathe me and through me. Breathe me and be me. My very lungs filling with Spirit. All I have to do is Be and I am filled with Light. I can feel the intake of Spirit and the exhale of Spirit. Into my world and into Eternity.

There are time when "I" am no more in the movement of atoms, cells and electrons and Spirit juice in and out, in and out, in and out. These moments used to be fleeting and I would worry that I would lose the sense of Presence by thinking about it. These days, the Presence is right there at every opportunity to creep in, flood in, leave me awash in the certainty of our merging together in the sacred marriage of the Ages.

Breathe me. And fill me. Allow me the chance to be fully me without encumbrance. Only the in and the out. From a place of the deepest calm I'll ever know. Cradled in Divine Essence. Ideas flash. Concepts coalesce. Words gather to poorly represent the inflow of an experience I don't fully expect to be given access to. Yet, there I am. Being breathed by my Soul. Nowing the Now. Unfolding the next moment and the nest and the next.

Hate for it to go away. Hate to come to the realization that I have strayed from my point of attention in the now to some thing in the future, or the past, or something wanted, or not wanted or many of the other distractions that I could be swept away by. "Just stay there", I say to myself, determined to savor the taste of Immortality.

10/25/14 Sequence of Events, as Noted, Beginning with Fear

- Awoke with a feeling of fear in my belly
- Recognized and told myself to Breathe
- Began to breathe and contacted HiC; let him in
- Within 10 Breaths the fear went away
- Had a strong feeling of HiC
- Began a conversation
- This is how healing can happen
- We're not doing Alice Baily work or anybody else's. Common man
- Always available. Up to me

- Merger is possible. Up to me.
- Was merged for a time
- Did Tai Chi with a love approach
- Could feel the merger and the Presence
- Healing of another, Sasha, happens when I am there and contact her HiC and we are hanging out together
- Healing occurs
- This is a way to heal in the future
- I want this more than anything. Up to We. HiC and me.
- Will require developing and staying very conscious
- Will not be like anybody else. Don't know anybody else
- Those in Spirit world want me to succeed. For all to succeed
- Keep describing the process, which may not have been done before in this way
- Blessed Be

SEE AUTHOR'S OTHER BOOK ON NEXT PAGES

HIGHER CONSCIOUSNESS SERIES BOOK 1

THE AMAZING BENEFITS OF MEDITATION

Living the Life You Want to Live

Health Joy Relationship
Creativity
Aliveness Stress Peace

BLAIR ABEE

The Amazing Benefits of Meditation Book

(This book is free if downloaded from this site, $.99 at Amazon. See below.) Recent scientific findings have confirmed what Master Teachers and mystics have known for centuries—meditation can help individuals in so many ways; meditation has many benefits–physical, mental, emotional, and spiritual.

Do you:

- Have a **stressful** life?

- Feel like you are on a never-ending **treadmill**?

- **Have physical, emotional, mental issues** you would like to address?

- Wonder what **inner peace** about your circumstances would feel like?

Do you want to:

- **Feel** better?

- Learn how to do **personal healing work** to address concerns and challengers you have?

- Improve your sense of **well-being**?

- Feel more in control of your mental, emotional, physical, and spiritual **health**?

GET FREE

The Meditation Book

Tired of meditation techniques that are frustrating?

- Meditation can be a difficult mind wrestling exercise.

- Want to use a meditation technique that is focused on Soul contact?

- One that is focused on Illumination rather than trying to tame the mind.

- Willing to try a simple yet powerful new meditation technique?

Would you like to:

- Be more **awake** and **aware**?

- Feel more **alive, joyful,** and **self-confident**?

- Experience more **peace** and **love**?

- Begin **healing** yourself   physically,   mentally, emotionally?

- **Attract** good **people, things,** and **circumstances**?

Book Available at Amazon Kindle in E-book and Paperback Form

PURCHASE NOW

Cover and title are being changed to <u>The Abundance Book</u>

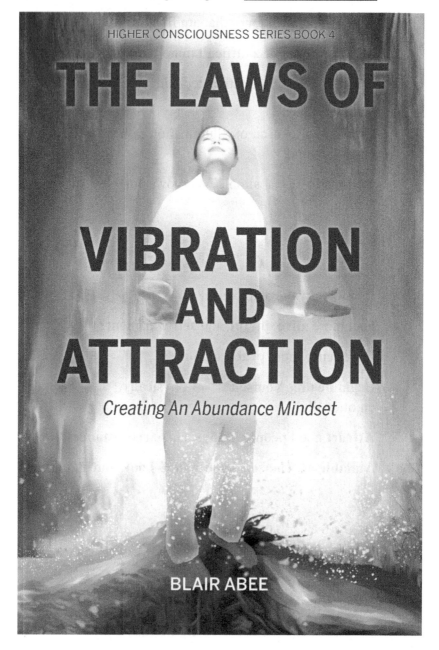

The Abundance Book, The Spiritual Path to Plenty

You were meant to live an abundant life, a life full of love, joy, peace, health, resources, and personal fulfillment.

Yet, we were all born onto a planet that is not easy to negotiate and which requires intelligence and cunning to create a sense of well-being for ourselves and for those we care about. Unfortunately, just getting through the day occupies much of our waking consciousness attention and personal fulfillment is illusive.

This book is an exploration of abundance and how the development of your spiritual side can help you experience your own, personal, true abundance.

The question of how to grow beyond a mere survival existence into a life of well-being has been the focus of many philosophers, authors, and spiritual teachers for centuries. Its most recent highly publicized exploration has been around the Law of Attraction and how to "have everything you want in life".

More fundamental than the Law of Attraction, however, is the **Law of Vibration**, which underpins the Law of Attraction. Also, more fundamental to having a new BMW appear in your driveway is the development of your Soul. It is your Higher Consciousness which generates the higher vibrations necessary to attract those experiences and things that support your personal growth and evolution.

The book explores twelve key principals and offers very specific instructions about how to activate the principals..

Explore the principals in this book and activate them for yourself. Your life will be so much more enjoyable when you do.

Book Available at Amazon Kindle in E-book and Paperback.

Purchase Now

HIGHER CONSCIOUSNESS SERIES BOOK 6

HOMAGE TO SPIRIT

Poems to Elevate Consciousness

BLAIR ABEE

Homage to Spirit

Do you like spiritual poetry? Revel in Rumi? Then you will love this **San Francisco Book Festival award winne**r. Every so often I get an urge to write poetry, and I just have to do it. Often it just comes pouring out. And I enjoy creating it as I read it. The **words just flow,** and they are almost always about a new realization I have about my spiritual unfolding. And unfolding and unfolding.

I never know what's going to unfold, until it already has. **Images come, inspiration leaps**, ideas flow out and onto the page, if I'm lucky enough to have paper around.

This book puts into verse many of the same ideas I have about humanity and the human condition:

- That **we are Eternal Beings** occupying very complicated biomechanical vehicles, but have come to identify with the vehicle, and its needs, that we have lost sight of who we really are.
- That the **stress, unhappiness, and suffering** we all experience, mentally, physically, emotionally, and spiritually **comes directly from that identification**, especially the identification with the on-board computer, the human mind.
- That we can **reclaim our true selves** through meditation and other techniques designed to interrupt the flow of the mind's running commentary.

The fear thoughts and attempts to control the uncontrollable unfolding of the Universe instead of cooperating with Spirit for Universal Good. **Book Available at Amazon Kindle in E-book and Paperback**

PURCHASE NOW

Made in the USA
Middletown, DE
27 October 2021